MAIR

FAIRMING

TALES

By

R.M.BAIKIE

Hope you get a bit
of pleasure from these books

Bert & Dorothy.

Printed at
The Orcadian Limited,
Hatston,
Kirkwall,
Orkney,
KW15 1DW

Published by
Bert Baikie,
Upper Ellibister,
Rendall,
Orkney,
KW17 2NZ.

2000

ISBN 0 9531564 1 9

CONTENTS

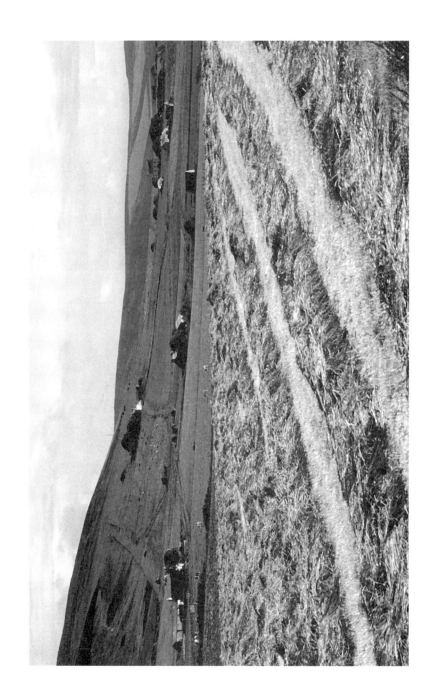

FOREWORD

If all Orcadians tried to save local stories and dialect as faithfully as Bert Baikie manages to do, we would once more be surrounded by our own warm accents, in our homes, in the streets, or even in school.

School teachers insisted that "English" was spoken in school. Our parents warned us that nobody (important!) would understand "wur wey o' spaekeen," so even they encouraged us to try this new language. Then we went to Kirkwall school to be mocked, because our accent was still very pronounced.

Exiled islanders returning home on holiday were praised if they "still minded the ald tongue," while those who succeeded to speak English (against their will!) shocked the locals to remark "no aaf twa meenits aund chantun every word."

We remembered scraps of stories told to us by our parents and grandparents. Now we wished we had listened "at the time, but hid's too late noo."

But suddenly it wasn't too late! Three years ago Bert Baikie published his book "Hid's Aal in A Day's Wark." That brought back many memories of similar things that had happened to us, or someone we knew. we were saying "Thoo must mind yin on. I'm younger than thee and I mind hid as clear as a bell!"

"Mair Fairming Tales," Bert's new book, is very cleverly

written, incorporating English and dialect stories and poems, with entertainment and amusement on every page.

We are given an interesting insight into former farming methods, combined with Orkney humour in different situations, and the modern worries over "permits" and "the man from Brussels!"

Orkney humour could be very witty, kindly, funny and at times "a bit beyond a joke." These tales will remind older folk of situations years ago, when they played a part in pranks, which they sincerely hoped the recipients never solved. Often however, the culprit was known. In one case, years later, a father lectured his son severely about his present day disgraceful behaviour at "Halloween." An old neighbour sympathised, saying, "Aye indeed, the rising generation hae no consideration. Hid's a blessing there's no ducks and scarfs to shove in trow folk's windows noo, no cairts and borrows tae hide and hardly ony lums left tae block wi strae, or thee son might hae been nearly as bad as thoo wir theesel, in thee young days!"

Reading this book, you feel you are there, watching each incident as it happens, like the "muckeen oot" of the byre with wheelbarrow, fork/shovel and elbow grease, then the final spurt to get the "loaded" barrow up the middeen plank. Rescuing the man who was stuck in the silage pit grass, up to the shoulders "with nothing more than a head to get a grip on." The rhodie cock who was hit "ahint the lug" with a stone. The escaped sheep that "got by me". The man who was "calfan his coo wi the spy-gless." You can clearly see the "twa muckle great men sittan apin the couples laek a pair o' stirlings, faired tae come doon!" Every farmer will sadly agree with the "modern" problems involved in "pittan oot the kye," and we all knew a farmer who could enjoy a joke on himself, because he was "that sort of a man."

Many of the stories originate in the "North Isles," Bert tells us. He assures me he was told the story on page 49 by a North Ronaldsay man!

"Don't judge a book by its cover," we are often told. In the case of "Mair Fairming Tales," we should, as the "cover" is a very accurate picture of the contents. Both have been very carefully produced by the author for our enjoyment.

B. THOMSON
Finstown

INTRODUCTION

In the three years since my first effort appeared on the local bookshelves, a good number of people have pressed me to write another selection of stories. This time I decided to simply record stories passed on to me by my fellow Orcadians. "There is a lot of scope for humorous stories from farming communities," one lady suggested, "base your work on these sort of tales, especially as there is so much gloom in farming circles today!" So this is an attempt to do just that.

In most cases I have tried to be discreet by making the sources and locations vague, e.g. North isles, which covers a vast area of Orkney's land mass, or West Mainland, East Mainland, etc. I am sure the people involved will be able to guess what or where the event refers to, and may even recognise themselves, or an episode in their lives.

In all aspects of life we can find humour if we take the trouble to look for it. This can take many forms, but it's often the innocent ordinary events which sometimes take an unforseen twist and can give us the best laugh when looked back on.

The lady trying to hold a conversation with a scarecrow for instance.

A wee boy trying to hide the body of a cockerel in the midden, after thinking he had killed it.

The elderly gentleman running into unexpected problems when 'answering a call of nature'.

All simple everyday events which because of unforseen circumstances turn an innocent everyday action into the realms of hilarious farce.

I can only thank the many people who, after reading my previous effort, came and told me their stories.

This selection is some of the more amusing and printable of these, which I hope will give the reader pleasure and enjoyment.

R.M.B.

ACKNOWLEDGEMENTS

Thanks to all the many people who passed on these tales to me in the first place, without them this could never have been published.

To Harald Nicolson and Fiona S. Nicolson for their illustrations - they are an essential part of the finished product, adding a subtle humour of his own to the text.

To Anne Cormack who corrected all the spelling and grammatical errors - once again!

Beatrice Thomson for her 'Foreword'. A local lady who knows and fully understands the Orcadian sense of humour.

The print staff of the Orcadian, they go out of their way to help get everything looking 'just right'.

I would like to dedicate this book to Brian Murray, of Stromness who has provided so much encouragement behind the scenes.

A RIGHT DAY O ID.

"Hid wis a day o id, that day whin the ould reed coo o wurs splet her tit on the fence." This the lady o the neebur hoose informed me wan day whin I hid stoppid by on some errand or ither. Wae hid been spaekan aboot some programme on the televeesion the night afore whaar a veet hid been haean a right strachle wi a coo that something hid gaen amiss wae.

I could see plainly be the leuk on the face o her that I wir aboot tae git the whole episode along wi me cup o coffee, so I linned back, straekid me legs oot afore the fire an waited for the tale tae unfold.

"Hoo can I ever forgit that day, 'id wis the day afore wur Kathy wis born! Thoo kens whut id's like at that stage, gaan waddlan aroond, aboot as much use as a stranded whale! The thing wis I wir sure I wir stairtan that morning, but didno waant tae say anything, or be runnan intae the ospital till things wis nearer tae hapnan". Sheu gaed her coffee a steer aroond reflectively, wi her spune, afore ga'an on.

"The kye hid no been oot for long, twa weeks or so, I wid say," she went on. "Charlie wis oot deuan something wi the sheep, I think, anywey hid seems that this ould coo got the notion that Ben wur dog wis gittan too near tae her calf, an meed a spret for the dog. Ben, paesable chap though he is, wisno gaan tae stand for that kind o impeedence fae any baes, he wheeled aboot an wi the biss aap meed a right gavse for the face o the coo.

Nixt Charlie kent, ould reedo wis maakan a spang ower the fence. Trouble wis, sheu didno mak a very good job o id, an got her hint end stuck apin the top wire."

Sheu paused for a sip o coffee before continuing her tale.

"Weel thoo kens whut happens in that kind o situation, the stoopeed oul thing yiggid an pulled till her legs wir free o the wire. They wir in a ferfal maes, aal cuts an scratches, an bluidan something terrible.

"Charlie gaed me a shout, an though I wirno for much use, wae managed atween is tae git her intae the byre an tied aap whar wae could hae a good leuk at the damage. That's whin wae noteeced that wan o the back tits wis splet so bad that the sides o hid wir jeust hingan wide aapen.

"Charlie leukid aap at me wi a ferfal serious face, "Goad lass wae can deu noathing wi that I doot, wae'll hae tae gae the veet a shout for this ane."

"So awey tae the phone he gaed, mutteran something aboot more needless expense.

"Weel, in less than a oor the veet wis at the door, ready tae see whut could be deun.

"Whin he saa the torn tit, he sheuk his heid. "Beuy Charlie

14

thoo his a bad ane there aa right," he commented, scratchan the back o his neck. "I think wae'll hae tae knock her right oot afore wae can deu anything wi that, as thoo can see sheu is gittan hersel in a bit o a state already".

"Whut he didno ken wis that sheu wis a ferfal fine coo at any time, but sheu wis terrified whin the veet's cam tae deu testing or anything o that kind. Sheu alwis gaed eum at the sight o wan o them."

Gittan tae her feet, sheu made her wey ower tae the coffee pot for a refill afore resuman her saet at the side o the stove.

"Noo whar wir I?" sheu windered, "Oh aye, I mind. Wur ould reed coo!"

"We'el thoo kens whut id's like tae knock oot a big baes laek a coo, thir's fairly big doses o stuff tae be injected intae them, than you hae tae wait a blink afore id works.

"Ken'an whut wur ould reedo wis laek tae inject anything intae, wae got a gate riggid aap tae try an jam her in the corner till the deed wis deun. Sheu snushed an gaed a bogle or two, rattled the gate wi her feet wance or twice, but that pert o the operation wis seun ower an deun wae.

"Sheu'll need a fifteen meenits or so afore id taks affect," Jeemie the veet informed is, "but id's no very clean here tae work wi her, is thir some better bit wae can tak her afore sheu goes doon."

"He gaed me a funny kind o leuk as weel, "An whut aboot thee lass, could I gae thee a jag as weel tae git thee gaan teu whin I hae me needle handy?".

"Dinna thee fash theesel aboot me, beuy," I says, "Aam fine as I am, "(though I wirno feelan as good as I wir twa oors afore, thir wis no wey I wir ga'an tae let on tae him)"

"The men hid a good leuk roon aboot an fund the ould drying green at the back o the byre. "Jeust the place wur needan," Jeemie stated, "wae'll tak her roond here on the rope whin sheus gittan middling groggy, an hid'll deu fine tae lay her oot on!"

"Weel thoo kens whut they say aboot the best laid scheme's o men an mice aa gaan agley, this turned oot tae be no exception.

"Whin ould reedo wis really waveran on the legs, Charlie teuk aaf her band, an wi the helter rope in his hands set for oot the door wi her. Goad kens whut happened than, wae don't!

"Whither something gluffed her at the door wae'll niver ken, but sheu gaed wan almighty bogle an teuk for aaf wi puir Charlie fair dirdan along the grund as he tried tae hing on. Hid aal happened so queek that nobody else hid a chance tae gae him a bit o' help.

"Wae did tae try tae hied her aaf, but hid jeust did more herm than good, an nixt wae kent sheu wis intae the slurry lagoon, right aap tae the shoothers. The trouble noo wis that sheu wis weel an truly stuck an could'no git oot. If sheu gaed doon under the effect's o the drug sheu wid smother, wae hid tae git her oot —-queek!

"The tractor wis fetched, an a strong (weel wae thout id anywey) length o wire rope. Jeemie the veet, cled in his waterproof claes, waded into the slurry an somewey or ither managed tae git the rope aroond her. Charlie got the ither end, heetchid id tae the back o the tractor an gently aised her ahied tae taak aap the slack. Slowly as he teuk the strain, the ould coo stairt tae move wi' Jeemie deuan whut he could tae help.

"Aal o a sudden there wis a fairfal crack an the rope breuk! In deuan so hid managed tae skelp Jeemie a right clipe ower the back o the hand. Beuy, beuy, whut a laek hand he hid efter!

Still he widno stop till he got the thing heetched aap again an finally got the ould coo oot o the iper. Whut a maes!

Beuy, thoo never saa—or smelt—the laek.

For a mercy thir wis a hose handy, an wae hid tae hose doon both man an coo afore anything else could be deun."

Sheu paused for anither swig o coffee afore continuan.

"You wida thout efter aal that the wounds wada gaen aal septic wioot a doot, but the surprisan thing wis that everything haeled aap as bonny an queek as if id hid aal been deun in the maist hygenic o condeetions.

"Aye, that wis truly some day o id I can tell thee that lass, wan wae'll no forgit in a hurry."

Weel warmed up be noo sheu hid anither sip o her coffee afore draan a deep breath again.

"Efter aal that cairry on, beuy thoo can imagine the maes that the claes wis aal in.

"Jeemie got a change o Charlie's tae pit on till he could git home again, an washed aaf the warst o the iper fae his own afore bunlan 'id intae the back o his caer.

"I hid tae deal wi Charlie's, as thoo might ken! Hid wisno fit tae pit intae the washer or anything laek that. Dis thoo ken whut I did wi the whole thing? I teuk the silage fork fae the byre an lifted the lot tae the burn an dumpid hid intae a hole there.(Hids a right mercy that the Environmental health folk wir no aboot or they wid haen me tae the coort for pollutan the burn.)

I deudno swill the claes aroond wi me hans for the waater wis so couled, so I cheust waded in an trampid id aal aroond wi me rubber beuts till maist o the dirt seemed tae be aaf. (Beuy hid teuk a lock o blotts tae git the smell o that iper aaf o everything.)

"Than I teuk id in tae run id throu the washer.

Hid wid been maist o a week efter that that wae could SMELL Charlie AFORE wae could see him, I wir cheust

17

affronted whin he cam intae the ospital tae see me an the bairn the nixt day."

"The nurse's wir on aboot the funny smell in the ward, an deudno ken whut hid wis. Bonny fine did I ken but I wirno lettan on.

Sheu glanced ower tae the clock on the mantelpiece, an sprang tae her feet. "Lord bliss me lass, is that the time, aal hae tae git the daenner on or Charlie'll be in afore hid's ready, an thoo ken's theesel hoo little patience he his for waitan.

"Thool come in bye again seun for anither blether will thoo no!" "Oh aye, aal deu that," I replied chucklan inwardly, thinkan that I hidno pitten in many words for the last half an oor anywey.

A WHOLE LOT O' BULL

"Dis thoo mind that 'Sharley' bull whut I haed a few ears ago?" Billo spiered me wan day at the mart.

"Yaas, beuy!" I answered, kennan fine that hid wis whut he wis expectan me tae say anywey, even though I hid no idea whut he wis ga'an tae come oot wi' nixt.

"He wis ower weel teu I suppose," he went on thoughtfully, a faraway leuk in his eyes, "but I got mesel a right fright wi him wan day oot on the field. Did I ever tell thee aboot that?"

Bonny fine did I ken that I wir gaan tae git the story anywey, even if I did say yes, so I meed id aisier for him be answeran, "No beuy, I don't think thoo ever did!"

There wis silence for a long meenit as he feenished tampan doon the 'baccy' an lightan his pipe. Aisan forward

19

to lean against the rail, he spat reflectively across the sawdust in the sale ring.

"Thoo kens yin field oot at the the back o wur steeding?" he started, "the wan wi that square bit fenced aaf i the middle o id!"

I nodded, tryan hard tae picture his place in me mind's eye, wioot hivan a lock o success.

"Weel that's the ould waell that wur watter supply comes fae," he gaed on. "Wae hae a big square o blocks built aroond id an twatree slabs o concrete laid ower the tap."

Thir wis a pause as he fired anither match tae rekindle his reluctant pipe. "Wae alwis thowt, thoo see's, that id wid be a haep safer wi a twa wires strung aroond, tae keep the baes awey, an tae keep fock fae runnan thir tractors ower the tap whin the fields bean rowt," he gaed on.

"Anywey, wan o the covers hid got broken in some wey a peedie while back, an I wir alwis gaan tae hae id fixed but hid never got roond tae id."

He paused and spat across the ring again. "Weel this day I thowt id wis time tae deu something aboot the thing, so I teuk me hammer, the chisel an a baer oot. I waanted tae see if I could prise the braken bits aap, tae let me ken hoo much I wir gaan tae hiv tae renew."

Wi a leuk o disgust on his face, he again carefully examined the once more extinct pipe afore stowan id awey in his inside pootch.

"Thir wis a lok o coos an thir calves i the field, an wur bull wis there amang them. They wir aal aetan awey tae the ither end o the field an payan me no heed as I waakid oot across. I wir chappan awey for a peedie blink whin something meed me leuk aap, an there at the ither side o the fence wis the bull!"

He sheuk his head. "I jeust kent be the leuk on the face o

20

him that I wir in trouble. He wisno happy wi me workan there, that wis plain tae see!"

"Whin he saa me leukan at him, he stairt tae snush an shaak is heid, makan funny moanan soonds. He stairt tae gae a scrape or two wi his front feet. Beuy, I could fin'd me kep risan apin the heid, for I kent thir wis no wey I could git oot o there an mak id tae the hoose. An I hid no tractor wi me."

"Whut did thoo deu beuy?" I speired.

"Hoo id cam intae me mind I don't ken, bit I hid a midleen heavy hammer in me hand, so I jeust drew back me erm an let id rip at him, is haerd is ever I could!"

"Beuy, id teuk im jeust fair an square atween the eyes. Aal swear they glazed ower for a meenit an I thowt he wis gaan tae go doon, for I saa the leg's om stairt tae bend, bit he sheuk his heid twa-three times an backid awey!"

"Efter a peedie blink he turned an gaed a'af. He steud in the faer corner o the field for a good while efter that. Believe thoo me, I teuk for the hoose whin I hid the chance. Nixt time I gaed back there I teuk the tractor wi me, an I meed sure the bull wisno in the saam field!"

"Did thoo keep him on efter that?" I asked.

"Oh aye he wis wae is for a couple o eer efter that, an I niver hid any bother wi him again. Whut teuk him that day aal niver ken! Hid most iv been me chappan wi the hammer that upset him. Or mibee id wis me grootan aboot on me knees that he didno understand. Bit as me feyther aye said niver trust a bull, no metter hoo paecable he seems tae be, they can change ferfal queek!"

AAP TAE THE SHOODERS

It is the way of all normal people, fairmers included, to go through life, consistently and unconsciously developing unique personal mannerisms. These habits we ourselves are totally unaware of, but they can give much quiet amusement to neighbours, friends, and acquaintances around us.

This tale is about a farmer living and working in one of the North Isles of Orkney, or so I have been told.

Typical of most farmers in the islands he liked to have his property neat and tidy, and it was a matter of pride on his part to keep things that way. It was also a matter of routine to have a regular look around the farm steading at a slack time, just to see that everything was in order.

Like a number of the older generation, his working claes included the inevitable 'kep', and the 'traditional' bib and brace dungarees.

Over the years this particular fairmer had got into the habit of shoving his hands deeply inside the 'bib' part of his garb whenever he was out inspecting stock, fences, or the like around the farm. This habit he himself was totally and blissfully unaware of, but it was widely noted as an individual idiosyncrasy by many who knew him. Little did he know that this very innocent little habit of his was to cause him one of the most embarrassing moments of his life. At the same time it was to consolidate for him a permanent place in the 'folklore' of the island.

This particular event took place late one afternoon in midsummer. His silage had been cut and stored the previous day by local lads, neighbours, who had set up a contracting business in the community. Having spent the bigger part of the day tidying up the bits and pieces of loose grass that had fallen over the sides, or had been missed by the buckrake, to his personal satisfaction, he set out on his usual tour of inspection. The obvious thing to look at in such a situation was the silo, so hands tucked away in their usual place he started to tramp around the top of his mound of newly consolidated grass.

Reaching the far end he crossed across to the other side to come back down along that one. Suddenly, without any kind of a warning whatever, the top gave way under his weight, and feet first he shot down into a hole inadvertently left by the 'buckrake man' who had pushed the grass in. It was not a very big gap really, just big enough for him to slip into, in his own words afterwards, "Laek a cork intae a bottle".

He was held fast, firmly wedged, right up to the shoulders.

So tightly was he trapped, that his hands were well and truly stuck, still firmly tucked into the front of his dungarees.

Not only that, but his legs too were so firmly held that he could not bend them to try to push himself upwards. He truthfully, "Could'na move a muscle!"

As any one in that sort of situation would do, he struggled to the best of his limited ability, in any way he could to try to push himself upwards, but all to no avail. He was firmly stuck, and having no other choice would simply have to wait until someone came to his aid.

When her hubby did not appear for his tea at his usual time, his wife began to wonder where he had got to. "He's never yeushally faer awey at maet times!" was her first thought.

After a time his failure to appear at the table finally began to get her worried. "Whut the devil's come o that man the night?" she wondered. "Is he lyan oot somewey wi a broken leg or something o the kind?".

Going out to the back door she gave him another shout, but hearing no kind of response, went back in to the house for her coat, before setting out a bit further to look around the out houses.

"His car's in the garage," she noted, "so he's no awey wi hid!" The tractor was in its usual place. There was no sign of him on the fields or among the cattle.

Despite repeated calling she heard no answer at all, and found no sign of life. Getting more worried by the minute now at this lack of response, she widened her search area until finally she thought she heard a faint shout for help.

Eventually after a lot of calling and searching, she discovered her hapless husband's head jutting above the surface of his own silage.

"Beuy, whut the devil ir thoo deuan stappid in there?" was her immediate reaction.

It was only when she came to try to help him out that she realised just how serious his position was. Try as she liked, she could do nothing on her own to ease his predicament. There was no other option, some of the neighbours would have to be called in to help.

With nothing more than a head to get a grip on, helping was not going to be easy, so a couple of forks were brought into play and carefully the silage was dug away from around the trapped man's shoulders until they were able to get a rope under his armpits.

Despite this, and putting forward the best efforts they could, they were still unable to move the helpless figure at their feet.

"Thirs noathing ither for id beuy, waell hae tae git the loader in tae aise thee oot o there I doot!" was the unanimous decision.

Again this took a bit of time, but eventually a tractor was eased into position, the ropes attached and slowly the hapless farmer was eased from his 'cell'.

Apart from a minor bruise or two from the rope, he was none the worse for his ordeal. His only comment at the time was, "Be-goad id wis some haet in there! Beuy's, I wir jeust in a drok o sweat aa the time, an most hiv lost half a stone in weight!" (Which considering his rather portly figure was probably no bad thing)

As the reader can no doubt imagine, it took this poor man a very long time to live down this escapade. The whole story when it became common knowledge in the district caused much hilarity among friends and neighbours alike.

Perhaps the story as it was passed on to me has lost bits or had parts of it embellished in some way. That after all would not be uncommon in a farming locality.

After all a good laugh at a neighbour's misfortune is one form of light relief in such a stressful lifestyle.

BEUY WHUT A MAES!

There must be few farmers out there who have never come off worst in an encounter with slurry equipment. Most will at one time or another have been coated liberally in this foul smelling 'end product' of present day farming, whether through mishandling equipment, or by mechanical breakdown.

A tale told to me recently typifies this beautifully.

An island farmer, who shall we say did not spend as much time as he should in cleaning and servicing machinery, decided that the time had come to 'aise' his slurry tank.

Out he goes and hooks up his tanker, ("Hid wis workan las time id wis yokid!") to the back of his relatively new four wheel drive tractor, and sets out to his job.

Now I do not know anything about the layout of his steading or how he went about loading up his tanker, but it did not take him long to do so, and head for the field with his cargo. On reaching the field the drive was engaged to build up the pressure in the tank, before opening the spreading control on the back of his machine. It was when he came to open this valve that he found it appeared to be stuck, and despite repeated efforts would not move.

After spending some time trying from the tractor end to release this, without any success, he dismounted from his seat and went to look at the machine itself to see what was wrong.

(Let me mention at this point that he had for many years had a problem with his eyesight, which meant that he wore glasses all the time.)

Not finding anything obvious wrong, he ventured closer, peering into the outlet nozzle. This appeared to be clogged with dried up dung, the leftovers from his last foray into the slurry tank.

Going back to his tractor, he searched about in the cab until he found what he thought was a suitable tool to help clear this blockage.

So intent was he on his task, he was completely oblivious to the fact that the tractor was still idling away, and the pressure in the tank was building up to its peak.

Back he went to poke and prod into the nozzle, trying to dig out whatever dried up obstruction was there. As is the habit of many who wear glasses, he opened his mouth as he peered into the dark recess.

I'm sure that you will have guessed by now just what happened.

With a resounding crack, the pressure from inside the tanker, combined with the prodding from outside, released the blockage and the slurry shot out with such force that the poor man was carried backwards on a jet of foul smelling semi-liquid.

His glasses were whipped off, his 'kep' went as well, and even his false teeth were dislodged from his mouth as the slurry hit the back of his throat and came out again.

No doubt it would have taken him some time to regain his balance, and clear his eyes again so that he could see enough to shut off the control valve.

Again no doubt he would have had to walk back to his home to get cleaned up, and get a change of clothing.

It would have taken more time to come back and search for his missing specs, cap and teeth, if indeed they were to be found at all.

In all there was half a day lost needlesly when a few minutes spent on giving things a wash down the previous time would have saved all this trouble.

The story I was told ended by stressing that he had felt ill for some weeks afterwards from the effects of the slurry he had swallowed.

It may be good for the grass, but it is not good for the human body apparently, especially when taken in undiluted form.

ANITHER SMELLY ENCOONTER

What it is about human nature that makes us laugh at the misfortunes of another? None of us would I suggest even have an answer to such a question, or even begin to understand.

If it were to happen to us, we would not think it the least bit funny, yet those around us laugh till the tears run down their cheeks.

A farmer of my acquaintance, running a one man holding, had been working for days on his own. He was washing down everything in his slatted byre, mixing the slurry in its tank, and spreading it on the field. Sunday morning came around, he felt absolutely 'knackered'(for want of a better word), and he still had not got his tank emptied. The weather was perfect for the job, but indications were that it was to break down very soon, and he wanted very much to get it finished.

He was very tired, and longing for a rest, so knowing that a young neighbour was free that day, and loved doing most farm related jobs, he gave him a quick phone call to explain the situation.

Sure enough this neighbour, let's call him Jock, was ready for a bit of action, and in no time he appeared to take over the work. He brought with him another neighbour Ron, who was always ready and willing to help out as well. So our farmer left them to get on with the job, knowing it was in good capable hands.

Very quickly they got to work, Ron on the mixer pump and Jock with the tanker taking the loads out to spread on the field.

All went well and soon the field was getting well covered in a satisfactory manner. Our farmer, making the most of his free time, was dozing in front of the television, taking the occasional glance out of the window at the activity outside.

On this one occasion however he noticed that the tractor and tanker were standing near the top of the field with Jock behind it. Next time he looked the machine was still standing, but there was no sign of the operator. Now the machinery was in pretty sound condition and there was little risk of major mechanical failure, so he did not worry unduly, knowing that his helpers were more than capable of sorting out anything in the machinery line, should there be any sort of problem.

Another quick look showed the machine still standing in the same place, but a movement nearer the end of the field made him look closer. What he saw was a sight he would not forget in a hurry. Jock was 'squelching' his way towards the house, covered from head to toe in slurry!

When the farmer went out to the byre to see what had happened, he found Ron almost hysterical with laughter, trying to wash off the worst of this foul smelling covering from Jock's clothing with a cold water hosepipe.

Through the fits of laughter he eventually learned the full story of what had taken place. Apparently a lump of hard slurry had avoided the mixer and been drawn into the tanker, and it had then passed through the valve at the back and blocked the nozzle.

Jock had then unwittingly opened up this assembly without closing the valve or releasing the pressure from the tanker, and got suitably decorated for his trouble.

Eventually Ron was able to subdue his mirth, at least for short periods to enable him to take more positive action.

He loaded the now bedraggled Jock into the boot of his car and set for home with him, to get him a change of clothing. Trouble was when they got there the poor chap was still in such a filthy state that he was unfit to go into the house. The solution was to strip down to his underwear before being allowed to enter.

His soiled clothing was duly dumped into buckets of water where it could be washed, until it was clean enough to be put into the washer.

Eventually, clean and shining, they returned to carry on with the work, but all the time he was working Ron gave way to torrents of laughter whenever the thought of Jock's slurry drenched figure came into his mind. Something like that can happen so quickly you have no time to think, but the consequences can haunt you for many years to come. This was one such event.

UP AND OVER

It's one thing to tell yarns passed on to you by other people, but like all the rest of you readers, this author too has had the embarrassment of an undignified 'come down' in life. It was back in the days before cattle were housed on slatted floors. Cattle of all ages were tied in individual stalls over the winter months, calves usually across from their mothers at the other side of the byre. In my case there was one calf that had been born around the festive season, and by March was a big strong beast.

Calves like this had been handled daily from birth and had no fear of people, so as they got bigger and stronger they could be difficult to handle. One morning after breakfast it was the usual feeding, mucking out routine in the byres, but first the calves were turned loose to suckle their mothers.

This first feed of the day was eagerly looked for by the calves, needless to say, and they were normally very lively.

As I came down the byres 'lowsing' calves as I came, the ones still left were getting more and more eager as their turn came nearer. When I came to the big one, it was practically prancing in its eagerness to get to work and I had some difficulty in restraining it until it could be loosed.

The moment it felt the pressure of its band easing it made one lunge forward, and shot right between my legs in its rush to reach its mother.

Now, as all who know me are well aware, I have suffered all my life from 'Ducks disease', (short legs, and a body not very high off the ground). So there I was, completely airborne, travelling backwards rapidly, and totally unable to do a thing about it!

As the calf shot up between the two cows in the stall, I was dislodged by two sets of none too clean 'rump steaks', slid over the calf's hind quarters, overbalanced, and landed in the night's supply of newly produced 'farm yard manure', on my back.

It was my luck that the cows were docile, many could have done a lot of damage by kicking at something unusual rolling about at their hind feet, but these ones ignored what was happening.

I was allowed to scramble to my feet as quickly as possible, totally unscathed, but extremely dirty.

It will not take much imagination by fellow farmers to understand the mess my clothes were in. It was a very simple case of get in for a change before completing the rest of the morning's work. Another of the joys of farming you could say.

This is the sort of occasion where a boilersuit really comes into its own. It may get dirty but it saves the rest of the clothes from a lot.

OOPS

This tale goes back into the distant past, when the farming life was so different from that of today. Back in wartime Orkney there was no such thing as a combine harvester, or silage, or anything like that. If you were lucky you had the use of a binder to cut the grain in harvest time. If not then you had to rely on the reaper or the scythe, and tie the sheaves by hand. It shows my age when I can say I have seen all these methods being put into practice.

Nearly every farm had a threshing mill of some sort to thresh the sheaves down when and as required. To help speed things up for those who wanted it, some parishes had an enterprising farmer with a travelling mill, willing to thresh down a number of stacks at one go. It was essentially a labour intensive operation, and helping hands from round the district would be called in for the day when a 'threshing' was on the go. This was a social occasion for all concerned, and despite the strenuous work the camaraderie and banter involved was enjoyed by all.

My story goes back to that period in the parish of Rendall.

Being early spring, one farmer had decided to thresh down some stacks of oats that had been standing in a field all winter, to get some seed ready for sowing when conditions permitted.

As it has been for centuries, where there was grain there were rats, and these stacks being riddled with tracks and holes ensured a large number of residents.

On this particular day as the work went on, scores of these furry creatures lost their warm winter quarters and had to flee for safety. There is little doubt a large number of them would have made it, though with every hand against them casualties would have been high.

One rather portly, elderly gentleman, Wullie, was on a stack with his fork, tossing up sheaves to the mill. He was well known to be a 'character' as they would say today, 'a very laid back' sort of person, nothing ever seemed to bother him unduly.

Anyhow as he was getting well down the stack another neighbour, Jeemie, noticed Wullie suddenly stop work, stick his fork into the top of the stack, and start fumbling with the band of his trousers. Before Jeemie's disbelieving eyes, out popped a big rat, which had apparently climbed up the inside of a trouser leg.

Refastening his garments once more, Wullie calmly lifted his fork and resumed work as though nothing out of the ordinary had taken place!

The young neighbour lad who had seen the whole thing take place, started to laugh, and laugh, and laugh until in the end he became so helpless he had to sit, or lie down, it struck him as being so funny. He swore he ached for days afterwards at the very thought of the whole episode.

I lose count of the number of times this tale has been relayed to me in the past, it is obviously one deserving a place in the annals of parish history.

WUR JEEMIE AN THE RHODIE COCK

Whin wae wir kids doon on the ferm,
Wae hid a Rhodie cock,
Hid wis a contramantious baes
This king o wur hen flock.

Wur Jeemie deudno laek him much,
For hid's this wey thoo see's,
Hid fleytered roond his ankles,
An dobbid Jeemick's knee's.

Wan day I mind, I mind id weel,
The cock hid gaed too faer,
Hid lighted intae Jeemie,
An gaed him a ferfal scare.

But this time Jeem's hid hin anof,
He picked aap a stone,
Drew back his erm an let her rip,
Than windered whut he'd done.

Id teuk the cock ahint the lug,
He drapped laek he wis shot,
Rolled on his back an closed his eyes,
Cheust ready for the pot?

Puir Jeemie thowt "Aam for id noo,
The folk they'll ken o this,
Aal find the weight o faither's hand,
He's no the man tae miss".

So driven noo be desperate need,
Tae save his quaik'an skin,
He grabbid aap the hapless burd,
The midden tae stap id in.

The deed complete, he steppid back,
An wip'id aaf the sweat,
His conscience clear he could relax,
Things tidied aap so naet.

A funny kind o skrekan soond,
Meed him tae wheel aboot,
The cock's heid raes abune the strae,
An wildly leukid oot.

Wur Jeemie thowt 'id wis a ghost,
An fled the graveyard site,
The cock raes aap tae his full size,
Than sheuk his feathers right.

Hid tottered roond on swayan legs,
An slowly sheuk id's heid,
Than staggered back amang his hens,
Tae pick an scrape an feed.

Puir Jeemick couldna understand,
Whut wey this cam tae be,
A died burd gittan aap tae wak,
Hids no a sight tae see.

Fae that day on baith cock an boy,
Kept ferfal weel apairt,
Each faird o whut the ither thowt,
No trouble wid they stairt.

But time gaed on an things did change,
The cock thraad hid's neck got,
Lost aal his bonny feathers,
An landed in the pot.

But Jeemick couldna aet a bite,
Hid fairly meed him bok,
Tae think tae aet apin a burd,
That he thowt wis a gok.

So that's me tale, ids fairly true,
Id happened long ago,
Whin men wir men, an boys got faired,
Whin cocks got aap tae crow.

A SHOT IN THE DARK

Another story from the past that I feel is worthy of a place in island history. Ok, so it's not really a farming tale, but as it happened in a farming community it earns its place for that reason alone I'm sure.

In the early 1940's, as most people know, Britain was at war, and though I have no memories of that time, there are still many among us who do.

There was a constant, almost daily, threat of invasion at any time during these early years. With the majority of fit, able bodied, men already involved in the war effort, those still left at home were drafted into what became known as the 'Home Guard', made famous on TV recently as 'Dad's Army'.

This motley group consisted of both the elderly and youthful, with an assorted collection of farmers, tradesmen, and even social misfits not acceptable to the forces in any other capacity.

Among the men in this community expected to be on hand to do his duty, was the Parish minister.

He was one of a rare breed of clergymen, a very down to earth individual, a true parishioner who was involved in every facet of life in his district. He even had the distinction of being one of the very few native born Orcadians to become a minister. A dedicated and popular man but, like so many educated men to whom books were tools of their trade, he was totally inept with any kind of mechanical appliance.

His fellow 'Guards' soon realised this likeable man was a much greater threat to them than any distant enemy was ever likely to be. They quickly learned that he was not one to be trusted with a firearm of any sort, in any circumstances.

Despite this the powers that be, in their wisdom (not to be questioned by mere mortals) decreed that he, like all the rest, was expected to do his share of training and other duties. There was no way of hiding behind his clerical collar when the welfare of the nation was at stake, was there?

One day the whole patrol had been out on a stretch of deserted moorland for some target practice, with their recently issued rifles. Before setting out, each man was given a specified number of rounds of ammunition.

The rule was that all unused ammunition had to be checked in and accounted for by the officer in command, that was very important.

It would never do after all for someone, on the journey back to his home, to go and 'bag a hare', with ammunition specified for the defence of the country, would it?

After returning to the 'hut' which served as their headquarters, each 'squaddie' was responsible for stripping down, cleaning, and then re-assembling his own rifle before inspection.

On this occasion someone's counting had gone wrong and

no one realised that our minister still had one 'up the spout', that is until he touched the trigger.

A deafening roar echoed around the confines of the small room. Simultaneously, or so it seemed, a resounding crash added to the noise as the stove pipe disintegrated, filling the room with soot ash, and chaos. The fire being lighted at the time, this was quickly followed by dense smoke billowing up from the glowing stove, filling every corner of the room with a choking cloud of pungent peat reek!

The hut was cleared in record time!

Not only did this 'rogue' bullet demolish the stove pipe, it also tore a gaping hole in the side of the hut as it passed through.

As any one can imagine, it took quite a lot of time and effort to tidy up the mess in the 'hut' and get everything repaired again.

I have been reliably informed that from that day on the minister was excused firearm duties, purely for the safety of the others in the platoon.

A PIG'S TALE

It was in one of the north isles I heard this tale, a rather gruesome one I suppose for the more genteel reader, but still part of the routine life for many, at least until recent times.

A couple of folk had, like many others, left behind the big city life in 'the sooth' and bought themselves a small croft on this island. Like many others, they slowly adapted to the much more relaxed pace of island life. In so doing they also got to know the many different ways and mannerisms of their fellow islanders.

Alf, let's call him that, was something of a craftsman. He enjoyed working and renovating the old out houses on the croft and soon the place was looking trim and cared for again. A few sheep, a few hens, and a couple of ducks, and he was happy and content with his lot in life.

Mabel his wife, too, was very good with her hands, and soon became involved with one of the local firms, producing fancy goods for their gift shop. This brought in a little cash to help pay for a few groceries and the essentials of life.

One day Alf had been called on to give a neighbour a hand with hauling his creels. While they were working, Mansie (let's give him a good Orkney name!) mentioned that his old sow had produced a litter of twelve piglets some time ago.

He was considering having them sent to the auction mart in a week or so to be sold. Anyhow by the time they set foot on shore again, Alf had agreed to buy two, one for himself and one for his father-in-law who lived nearby.

These pigs grew and thrived, as they do on the care and attention meted out to them. Summer progressed, and in what seemed a very short time they were considered 'ready for the freezer'. Two to be killed at one time though was considered a bit too much for one household to handle, so one was duly disposed of in the usual manner. Just routine work in an island community really. The second one was left for a week or two, before it too went the way of its brother.

Then fate took a hand. The regular island 'slaughterman', Tam, became ill and had to go to the local hospital for a lengthy stay. The pig grew on!

This second reprieve was no doubt appreciated by the pig at least. He grew bigger!

On Tam's return to the island, he still needed a number of weeks to recuperate before resuming his normal life. The pig grew bigger still!

For the benefit of those who do not understand island life, let me explain. In any island there are people who are called on to perform routine tasks for the community in general. There is one individual who is therefore called in to slaughter things such as a pig, or a sheep or lamb for the freezer. Perhaps an animal that has had an accident or the like, is in pain and needs to be put down in a humane fashion. There is usually one islander who has the necessary skills to deal with this.

When this person meets with a mishap, or when illness strikes, as happened to Tam, there is an immediate problem for the whole community, unless someone else can take on this task. In this case there was no one in the community capable of taking over!

The pig grew bigger still, and the size was becoming the talk of the community! So much so that islanders out for a Sunday run would drop in past the croft to admire this giant 'porker'! Cameras were produced and people had their photos taken with this 'celebrity'. By the time Tam had got back to fitness once more, Alf's gigantic pig had become something of a celebrity on the island.

Eventually the day dawned for the 'evil' deed to be done. Word travelled round the island and first one local, then another, rolled up in whatever transport they had available.

Soon the croft was surrounded by vehicles of every kind, colour and description. Not only that, but the majority had brought along whatever kind of 'refreshment' they had available. In no time at all there was an atmosphere about the place the like of which had never been seen on the island in the lives of any of the inhabitants.

With so many people around there was not enough work for everyone, so someone produced an accordion, a couple of fiddles appeared from somewhere else. The party atmosphere took over as the music and the 'spirit' of the occasion began to work its magic on the gathering.

By the time the various parts of Alf's by now deceased pig had been sorted out, there was one of the best going parties the island has ever known, taking place. On and on into the night it went, and only when daylight came in once more did the assembly start to disperse to their own homes.

The 'celebrations', and their after effects, have been long spoken about since that memorable day.

One lad sitting, rather the worse for wear, at the back of the buildings wondering if the contents of his churning stomach were to take the upper or lower route of release!

Two brothers walking unsteadily along the road ran into trouble when one fell into the ditch. Wedged firmly on his back he was unable to rise. "Gies a hand beuy," he implored his brother, who duly obliged, but pull as he liked he could make no impression.

Only when a neighbour came along did he find out that, in order to get a good grip on his brother's arm, he was at the same time bracing a foot against the unfortunate man's rib cage. Little wonder he was having problems.

Another who had been having a 'good' night, kept falling off his bike on the way home. He swore someone had been tampering with the brakes, which from time to time seized up solidly and threw him off!

The following day someone else returned to look for the false teeth which he could not even remember losing.

Some time later two of these who had been there, were discussing the event. "Beuy, that wis some night o id, wis id no?" one commented.

"Yaas min," the other agreed, "Aam been at miny a waer waeddin in me time!"

IT'S A CLEAN ONE! HONEST

Two Ronaldsay men were great cronies, and rarely a day passed that they did not get their heads together to chat about anything and everything of interest happening in their community, or elsewhere.

One night Robbie appeared at Jeemo's door, to be met by Edith, Jeemo's wife, who informed him that his friend was in the bath having a good scrub as they were planning to go to Kirkwall the following morning.

So Robbie settled himself into his favourite chair to wait, with the traditional mug of 'home brew' at his side.

Eventually a glowing Jeemo appeared from the direction of the bathroom.

"Aye min, I hear thoor been waeshan thee hide wi Tide!" Robbie greeted his buddy jokingly.

"No beuy," came the quick reply, "aam been waeshan the baa's wi Daz!"

Picture the scene, a typical West Mainland farm, a well run family unit with a traditional father and son partnership. They were not all that much into the latest in machinery and housing ideas, more you could say being reluctantly forced into newer practices by outside circumstances. Still, despite those traditional sentiments, they were no different from others in the farming line. For them as with anyone else, trouble in one of its many forms can strike at unexpected times.

This time it was well into the spring, and new calves had been arriving regularly over the past five or six weeks. Space was getting very cramped as every stall and odd corner was filled with new calves and their mothers. Bad weather meant that the fields were not dry enough to turn out the young cattle that had spent months indoors, which would have eased greatly the pressure on space.

With most of the older cows now calved, there were only a few heifers still due, and they were being watched carefully. A visit to the byre in the middle of one night, showed that one of these was about to calf. She was having a bit of a struggle on her own and needing some help, so to be on the safe side, the other male member of the household was called from his bed to give assistance. To give them room to work more freely, the heifer was coaxed, reluctantly, into the half empty barn.

Eventually, after a lot of sweating and straining on the part of all three, a good strong calf was delivered and the men stood back to admire their handiwork.

The new mother was not in the least impressed. Perhaps she blamed those two humans for all the pain and discomfort inflicted upon her, so scrambling to her feet at speed, she 'went for them' with obvious enthusiasm.

Only then did they discover that she had their only means of escape well covered. To reach the door, and sanctuary, they had to get past this by now enraged heifer, at serious risk to life and limb. The only safe haven was a pile of bales stacked along one wall, so up they went — at speed!

Seeing her quarry escaping, the heifer then vented her anger on the bales, causing the men to grab hold of the roof timbers and haul themselves on to the couple backs in the hope that things would soon quieten down again.

This young mum was no fool though, and as she tended her new born calf, managed to keep an eye on 'the enemy' and thwart every effort on their part to escape from their perch. How long they would have had to spend there we will never know, if fate had not decided to sort things out in its own way.

The lady of the house, lying awake, wondering what was keeping her men-folk out for so long, decided to investigate. Finding a peaceful byre with no-one there she was attracted to the barn door by a faint sound from the other side.

The scene revealed as she opened the door can best be described in her own words. "There wis this peedie ting o a quoyo staan among a rummel o bales, lickan awey apin her calf, an twa muckle great men sittan on the couples laek a pair o stirlings, faired tae come doon!"

This timely form of distraction broke the stalemate though, and perhaps the heifer had by now calmed down a bit.

Maybe now with her attention split three ways, she decided that the calf was her priority. Who knows, but when the men very cautiously lowered themselves down from their lofty perch and hastily scrambled for the door, she barely glanced in their direction.

Needless to say they will remember this lesson for a long time, it always pays to have a handy escape route at such a time, in case of emergency!

TREU THE LEUKAN GLESS

Farmers, perhaps more than most other trades, are experts at adapting and using anything and everything that comes to hand, in ways no other person would ever contemplate. It's little wonder then that these poor Health and Safety Inspectors are sometimes driven to despair by some of the ingenious 'inventions' they come across in their dealings with the farming community.

This tale though has little to do with such things, but it shows how necessity can lead to eccentric behaviour at times, and how otherwise sane and sensible people can be driven to use whatever is at hand to cope with everyday problems.

Jock was at a sale in the Mart one day, and like most farmers, enjoying a yarn, but keeping a weather eye on the sale ring for any chance of a 'bargin'! One Monday he succumbed to the temptation of putting a bid on a cow in calf, which he thought was cheap. When no other bid was forthcoming he found himself the new owner of a cow he really had little need of. Still, having bought her, he was obliged to take her home.

It was when he got her there that the true nature of his 'cheap' cow showed itself. To put it into his own words "Sheu's a wild divel, right anof, no safe tae be aboot hands wi at aal!"

Time passed and as dark winter days eased into spring, Jock's cow grew bigger and bigger as she came nearer to calving.

Her temperament had not improved in any way, and she needed to be handled carefully at all times. With every passing day, he got more and more worried about how he was going to deal with her in his cramped byre if she chose to calf in the middle of the night. Though he would never ever have admitted it even to himself, Jock was, in the farming term, 'faered for her'!

So worried was he getting to be that some nights he slept hardly any. His despairing wife was being driven to distraction by the pair of them, "Why dis thoo no pit the d——d thing tae the Mart, an git rid o her?" she would say, "than thoo might git some paes tae sleep at night, an so could I!" But Jock was dogged like so many Orcadians, and not the one to give up on a 'bargin' as easily as all that.

Finally Jock got a fine day, and his cow and two or three others were unceremoniously herded out on to one of the fields near the house. Again the cow was being watched tightly, but this time from the safety of long distance.

But not only was the cow being watched, Orkney being Orkney, it meant that Jock's eccentric behaviour was quickly noticed by first one, and then another of his neighbours.

The local 'bush telegraph' took over and soon the whole district was taking a keen interest in "Jock's coo".

Every movement on the farm was noted and passed from one to another, and soon the welfare of his 'wild coo' became the number one topic of conversation.

This cow finally came to her 'big day' and like many another in similar situations drifted to a far corner of the field to be away from her compatriots. Not unusual behaviour for any cow in this sort of situation, in fact it is pretty well normal for most.

About this time, another of Jock's neighbours, Robbie, was heading for the local shop for his weekly supplies, and that necessity of life, his Orcadian.

Passing the next door house to Jock's, he spied Jeemie the

elderly owner seated in his favourite chair out in front of the house, enjoying the fine morning sunshine and his pipe.

Robbie stopped for a blether, as neighbours do, and they covered many topics of the local gossip and scandal in a very short time.

Noticing that now and then Jeemie's attention seemed to be wandering, Robbie soon became aware of the cause.

Jock was popping out of the house every few minutes to stand at the corner, apparently shading his eyes, and gazing into the distance.

Never one for the subtle approach, Robbie was quick to ask, "Whut the divel is Jock deuan the day?"

Jeemie, in the middle of lighting his pipe, took his time to reply, "Aam no right sure beuy!" he said, "But I think he's oot there calf'an his coo wi the 'spy-gless'!"

THE WAN THAT GOT AWEY

As most people in a farming community know only too well, some sheep are obsessed with looking for 'fresh pasture'. This is usually on the 'other' side of the fence which is supposed to keep them in a field. Almost every farmer with a flock of sheep has, among them, one rebel who will find a way out of the best of fences. As one farmer was once heard to remark to a crony, "I could big a waa roon the field, an pit a leud api the tap, an the oul div'l wid still git oot!"

One such adventurous creature took up residence on a neighbour's farm. To get there she had to cross a boundary ditch, with substantial fences on either side, separating her from her cronies. Days moved on into weeks and she duly produced a single lamb. The pair of them grazed happily on the lush grass of spring, only returning to their own home territory when the owner of the land appeared with his dog or his tractor, to work on this field or a neighbouring one.

In time she grew in confidence, if that was possible, and wandered further and further into the neighbour's land. On moonlight nights she explored further, returning to the same field as daylight dawned again. Life was good and she and her lamb were thriving on the plentiful pickings.

With growing confidence however, as many of us know, there can also come complacency. This cocky old lady was no exception. Her boldness became her downfall, so ending for her the good life she had enjoyed for so long.

During their nocturnal excursions, the pair had discovered the farmhouse garden, and as sheep will, sampled what was on offer there. This supplement to their diets was greatly appreciated by them, but their unfortunate hosts did not value these visits to anything like the same degree. War was declared, and the truants found themselves being unceremoniously chased back to their owner's property whenever they were sighted. This state of open hostility went on for days, and could have lasted a long time, if fate had not decided to take a hand.

In typical Orkney fashion, a severe storm came blasting in from the north one evening. All night it blew in heavy sleet and snow showers which carried on well into the morning. The farmer, doing his rounds of the steading, giving the cattle their morning feed, discovered a shed door had blown open during the night, and closed it as he went past. Later in the day as the weather abated, he went to this shed for some purpose, and discovered he had unwittingly captured his two unwanted guests.

"Right," he thought, "Aal keep ahad o them noo an gae ? (I don't remember the name) a call an let him ken whar they aar, he'll mibee tak them home or pit them tae a different place!"

This was duly done and routine duties were resumed.

Later in the day the farmer was out with his tractor trying to finish a bit of ploughing. He saw his neighbour with a very useful looking van heading towards the house. Knowing that they were acquainted with which shed the animals were in, he carried on with his work, leaving them to it.

It was with shocked disbelief a few minutes later that he spied a small white animal heading at high speed across his field. When it came closer he saw it was the lamb. Head down, wild eyed, and with legs pumping like the pistons of a racing car, the lamb never slowed down as it approached the boundary. At full speed it dived through the fences and over the ditch, to disappear into the heart of the flock as if all the devils in hell were after it!

A few minutes later, the van appeared coming up across the field and a rather 'sheepish looking', shall we say, farmer emerged. With his teenage son sitting in the passenger seat grinning at his father's embarrassment, he had to admit that one of the prisoners "hid got by them!"

"Aam taakan the ould yowe wi me," he stated. "If the lamb comes back tae leuk for her, wad thoo close the door on id an let me ken!"

"Fine that beuy," the farmer replied, "Wad thoo laek me tae pit a bit o rope apin id as weel for thee!"

(He couldn't resist throwing in this comment)

"Aye, aye!" came the dry response, "no need tae rub id in!"

If the lamb ever did return, it must have been in the middle of the night as it was never seen again on the farm. As for the ewe, she too never appeared again. On inquiring about her one day much later, the farmer received the rather caustic answer, "Sheu's in the freezer beuy, aam no seen wan coman oot o there yit!"

WHUT A LOAD O S—T

Young people working in farming today, with machinery doing all the work, have missed out on many things their ancestors took for granted, and looked on as routine duties. One such would have been the daily chore of byre cleaning.

Or perhaps to put it into today's 'yuppie' jargon, "removing recycled organic matter from the cowshed".

Who among the older generation still around can forget the wooden wheelbarrow, heaped to overflowing with nature's end product and staggering out, from a lighted byre into semi-darkness, to aim the solitary wheel in the direction of an unseen wooden plank.

I think there's a fairly good chance that no-one who has done so, and is reading this today, will have managed without coming to grief at some time or another.

To wheel a fairly heavy load up a sloping plank needs initially a fair degree of not only strength, but also momentum. If you managed to hit the plank at speed, you could put your load high up on the midden before dumping it.

Tipping it lower down meant taking a fork and 'haevan back the mideen' when you ran out of 'couping' space.

Small farms could usually get by with a single plank to serve their needs, others needed two, and the bigger places sometimes had more to negotiate on a big midden.

As if this were not enough, there was then the vagaries of the weather to make the job even more 'interesting'.

Winter here in the north can have a whole lot of nasty little surprises in store for the unwary!

As we all know, it rains on more days than anything else.

But rain as we all know comes in so many guises, from light to heavy drizzle, to heavy downpours, sometimes falling straight down and at others coming towards you in a horizontal direction, borne on a typical winter gale.

This constant pattern of wetness, coupled with a total lack of 'drouth', means that the plank in the midden was seldom dry.

Not only that, but in time a slightly greasy, slimy deposit starts to accumulate on the surface. Combine that with a boot sole which is 'past its best' and you have a heady combination, ready to give the Health And Safety boys palpitations.

Then there is the wind, that great unpredictable element of our weather. We all know how that swirls and eddies around buildings, or over roofs and seems to come at you from two or three different directions at once, upsetting your balance despite your best efforts to remain steady.

Given the right combination of swaps and swirls, you could be almost bodily lifted from a plank complete with loaded barrow. Add to that heady mixture a sprinkling of snow, or even a good going blizzard, and you were faced with yet another completely new challenge. Chances are though that you would see the outline of the plank better after a light snowfall, as it would be the smoothest, whitest part of the midden.

Give it a coating of grit or 'hen-sand' and you could do fairly well at getting up the midden still.

The real killer, though, was that morning and evening scourge, the black ice. A coating of that could be on the plank and you would never even be aware of it until your feet shot off in some totally unexpected direction, with the usual consequences.

There's more than one of us landed face first in this smelly 'end product of nature' in such circumstances. Mercifully for most, a quick wash down was all that was needed to make us presentable again. Occasionally though you would hear of someone unluckily getting a broken leg or arm, or probably a strained back as a result of these mishaps! But thankfully such injuries were few, though they did take some time to mend.

Then again such simple things as 'gaan squint' half way up the plank, could mean a foot and leg sinking to knee or thigh in the not very firm contents of the midden. A dropped barrow could roll back on such an occasion, pushing the unfortunate victim deeper into the mire.

Yes, today's farmers have missed out on one of life's true experiences in their quest for mechanisation, but then perhaps today's methods are more practical. One of these situations where getting further away from 'nature' could be said to be a good thing.

On a very few farms now the 'dung barrow' is still an essential part of the winter equipment, but the plank has disappeared from most places, to be superseded by the tractor and loader which can 'big aap the mideen' in a very short period of time.

'Couping' is usually on to a concrete midden floor these days, and while ice can still be a problem on the odd day it's not a major one any more.

But a passing thought to any of today's Young Farmers Clubs looking for an idea for a competition. How about a load of 'you know what', a wooden plank and a midden?

It would be like 'It's a Knockout' with interest, and could be a real crowd puller!

How I would love to be there with a video camera to record the action! Wouldn't you ?

PEST CONTROL

He had lived on his own in an isolated hill croft ever since the death of his elderly mother many years before. Never wealthy, he had enough to get by on, and was content with his lot. "Twatree yowes, twa coos, an a pucklie o hens" was his livestock.

The sheep produced lambs from time to time, the cows had their offspring, and the hens produced eggs which could be sold or eaten. They too occasionally came along with a few chicks to keep the numbers up.

His farming methods tended to be rather haphazard, rough and ready, or whatever other expression you might want to use. But on the whole he was happy living as he did in a situation where he was nearly at one with nature. Nature however did tend to try to take over at times and had to be firmly put back in its place, by whatever means the situation required.

Rats were the bane of his life, coming in as they did from their breeding grounds out among the heather. They would congregate in his stacks, to live on the grain crop he had grown the previous year.

"Big anes teu, wi eyes like geeg lamps!" was a favourite expression. "Wild b——rs teu!" he would add.

They got into the byre, the barn, and even took eggs from his henhouse if the opportunity arose.

But they were not the only predators to raid his henhouse. Others came in on wings, stealthily and silently, in quiet moments when no-one appeared to be around.

Watching from the window of his living room one day, he saw the winged visitor descend, land in front of the henhouse, glancing furtively around as he shook out his black feathers. Apparently satisfied there was no danger, the visitor calmly entered through the small opening placed there specifically for the use of the hens. In a very short space of time it reappeared with an egg in its beak, and calmly flew off with its prize.

Now this farmer was well known in the district as something of an expert with his rifle, so he vowed that he would have his revenge next time this happened. Next day he went about his duties as usual, having slipped his trusty weapon into a suitable vantage point in the shed the previous night under cover of darkness. Leaving nothing to chance he took the precaution of collecting all the eggs into his bucket before returning to the house, sure that his every move was being watched from a distance. Moving to his shed he took up his position and waited.

After what seemed to be half the morning, the black wings once more flapped down in front of the henhouse, very warily as though detecting some hint of danger. With a flurry of wings it flew off again and circled around, landing this time on top of the house, all the time keeping a nervous lookout. Before the farmer could get the time to adjust his position in order to line up his sights, the bird flew off again, this time to stay away.

Next morning, the farmer was woken by loud cackling from his henhouse, and on going to the window was just in time to see the egg thief emerge and take off with yet another 'prize'.

His rifle was still of course waiting in the shed where it had been left the previous day.

Night time came and this time he closed the opening on the hens' house after they were all inside for the night. Again when morning came he was ready, went out and fed the hens, opened the hole in the side of the house for them and went back in for a belated breakfast. The rifle had been taken in the previous night under cover of darkness and was now waiting alongside the open window of his bedroom. This time the faded curtains were drawn fairly tightly across, leaving only a very small gap at the bottom.

Sure enough a flurry of wings announced the arrival once more of the predator. Confidently it landed and strutted toward the henhouse, cawing in apparent contempt as it glanced towards the farmhouse. It was the last sound it was ever to make. The rifle spoke its message of death, and the crow slumped to the ground. Victorious, the farmer went out to claim his prize, to hang it up as a stark warning to others who might have been watching and waiting for such an opportunity.

While he was there he thought he may as well collect his eggs also. It was when he reached up to lift his bucket from the nail he had left it hanging on, that he discovered many were smashed. Apparently the bullet, passing right through its target, had struck a stone, ricocheted through the thin wooden panel of the house and right through the bucket containing the eggs. He never again left his egg bucket hanging in the henhouse.

A RIGHT LITTLE 'B'

We all know the type, these obnoxious little boys between the approximate ages of six to ten, who invariably are around to make a nuisance of themselves whatever is going on. Some of us have no doubt at one time been considered to be such by others, and are completely and blissfully unaware of that stigma as we move on into adult life. But when the time comes around that any little 'B' gets 'put into his rightful place', someone is inevitably around to pass on the tale to the rest of us.

Many years ago an island farmer had two sons. There were quite a few years of difference between their ages, and in character they could not have been more different. The oldest lad was a pleasant well mannered, very helpful young fellow, highly thought of by friends, neighbours and relatives alike. The younger from his earliest days proved to be a real handful for his parents, a torment to his long suffering brother, and had the distinction of being branded 'a right little B' by no less a person than his own father!

He was around, making more of a nuisance of himself than usual, when a squad of builders came to the farm to put an extension to the byre and midden. In his eyes this was his God given opportunity to really make a name for himself.

For days he had tormented and harried the workers until they were all heartily sick and tired of the sound of his boyish treble. The older son, despite his brother's tormenting, was proving his worth, helping with many small jobs around the site, and was a favourite with the squad. Probably jealousy by this favouritism meant the elder brother soon became the victim of much more than normal of his brother's pranks.

One day he was showing off as usual, and scrambling along the top of an old midden wall which had still to be taken down. Suddenly a rather fragile part wobbled under his foot, and with a piercing yell he disappeared from sight. When the first of the workers appeared on the scene, he took one look over the wall and started to laugh at the sight he saw before him. The lad had not only landed in the softest place he could, it was also the dirtiest part where the run off from the midden was. He had overbalanced, not only going full length, but rolling over as well as though to get even more liberally coated. He was black, he was wet, he was smelly, and the line of laughing faces he looked up at made him feel no better.

He disappeared, and was not seen again that day. From then on he was much more subdued when the workmen were around. If he got cheeky, or too full of himself, the threat of being dumped over the wall was enough to calm him down, to behave as one of the men put it "Like a normal boy".

A SKROO WI A TWIST

A young servant man on a ferm in the west,
Whut a cocky wee lad, he kent he wis the best!
Whitever the job deun be anywan ither,
Wis scornfully mocked, they cheust shouldno bother.
Whin this maister craftsman arrived on the scene,
Nobody else hid a right tae be seen.
His confidence oozed oot like sweat fae his pores,
As he swaggered aroond, gittan on wi the chores.

But as wae aal ken, pride at times taks a faa,
Whin wae laest expect id, wur back's tae the waa.
This brettan wee chap noo, he wisno immune,
The day cam aroond whin he teu wis cut doon.
Hid happened wan day i the middle o hairst,
Thir wis shaevs tae be cairted, aye this wis thir first.
The boss set them aaf wi the steeth o a skroo,
Than steud back an says "Can thoo hannel her noo?"

He wis gittan weel on, no so good on the pins,
But liked tae be oot there, tae supervise things.
So 'Cocky', as ever, squared aap tae the task,
"Aal big aap thee skroo!" said afore he wis asked.
" Ir thoo sure o that?" the boss speired wi a smile,
"No bother, aam deun id a minys the time"
The truth wis that though he hid been aboot hands,
He hid niver afore din more than tie bands!

Still he raise tae the challenge an gave id his best,
An rasseled an placid the shaeves till he whessed.
As the stack grew in stature, he scorned all advice,
Aboot whut he should do tae keep id aal nice.
But the man on the grund could see things wir gaan glide,
An the side o the skroo wis near ready tae slide.
Whin he hid a spare meenit, he stuck in a prop,
An than fund anither, the problem tae stop.

"Thoor gittan too high beuy!" the man shouted aap,
"Haal the shaevs in aboot thee an git tae a tap!"
But wur cocky wee sparra he didna ken hoo,
Tae tak the shaevs in for the tap o a skroo.
So shaef efter shaef still he placed him aroond,
Than the side slippid oot, an he sank tae the grund.
He didno git hurt for the landing wis saft,
As the rest o the folk steud aroond there an laughed.

Despite his auld legs the boss than steppid in,
Sorted oot aal the maes an bund the shaevs in.
In no time at a he hid a fine skroo,
Wi a fine shaepid tap, a joy tae the view.
A real work o art, laek whut they can be,
Whin a craftsman sets oot tae shaa whut he can dae.
Poor 'cocky' as if tae atone for his sins,
Wis sent back tae the steading tae feed the auld hens.

HOO ID YEUSED TAE BE

For the younger generation of today things like telephones, electricity, and water at the turn of a tap, are taken so much for granted, it is difficult to imagine life without them. In the past things were so different. These things just did not exist.

There was no such thing as an inside toilet as we of today are used to, unless the 'peedie hoose' in the garden qualified for that distinction in a few rare cases.

Even if it did the common users of that facility were normally the female members of the household, while the males, of the farming community at least, used the byre to answer calls of a natural disposition. That old standby, the 'chanty' (or 'chamber pot' as it is more widely known) had its own secluded place in the bedroom, for night time emergencies only of course.

This tale comes from that dim and distant era.

Few of us have experienced the hardships of these 'less enlightened' times. There are still some who have memories of parents or grandparents talking of that 'different world' so many of them lived through in their youth.

Let's just call him Fred. He was an elderly crofter, with the usual tidy cluster of farm house and out buildings lumped together tightly in the style so common at the time.

Fred was sitting relaxing after his day's work. Feet 'straiked' out in front of his old Enchantress stove, its top glowing a dull red in response to a good fill of dry peat. With a pipe full of walnut plug he sat scrutinising his Christian Herald, by the light of the old Tilley lamp hanging from a hook in the ceiling.

As time wore on he became aware that one of these routine calls of nature needed immediate attention. Getting to his feet, he tore off a sliver of paper, stuck it between the bars of the stove to get a light, and set it to the wick of his lantern. Placing the inevitable cap on his head, he set out for the byre.

When he reached there, the lantern was hung in its usual place, a hook shaped piece of wire hanging from a couple back. Quickly he settled down to his task, in his normal place.

In the stall alongside was a big, rangy, stirk. Like all the cattle in the small byre, this one was very docile, and like most cattle, curious. He was aware that it was not usual for Fred to be coming into the byre at such a time as this, so swallowing a mouthful of cud he leisurely got to his feet.

As cattle do, he then allowed himself the luxury of a leisurely stretch. He was still not comfortable, and stamped his foot to ease the discomfort in his hind leg. After lying in a rather cramped stall for some time, he had 'pins and needles', so taking his weight on the other three he shook the offending leg out behind him.

It was then he discovered that his foot had caught in something, something which seemed to have twisted around his ankle. He shook and jerked the foot to rid it of this obstruction, unaware that it was Fred's loose dungaree straps which had got entangled.

Poor Fred was, to put it mildly, in a predicament! With his garments in disarray, he could not regain his feet, or his balance because of the wild jerking. He was helpless as he rolled around on the floor of the byre until the stirk finally managed to free its foot.

It goes without saying that it was a rather dishevelled, dirty, and embarrassed Fred who returned to the kitchen a few minutes later. Even his cap had been 'decorated' liberally with the contents of the 'cester'.

"Beuy, whut the divvel ir thoo been deuan, tae git intae siccna a maes?" demanded Maggie, his wife as she spied her bedraggled spouse coming through the door. It was a long time before she was able to speak again, as the true picture came to light. She laughed and better laughed, until as she told a crony afterwards, "I thowt I wir gaan tae end mesel."

So helpless was she that Fred had to attend to his own needs as far as cleaning up was concerned, and it's not the easiest of jobs scrubbing the middle of your back with a cloth and getting rid of the sort of dirt he was covered in. Outer and under garments, all had their fair share of nature's bounty, and everything had to be changed. By the time he had got reasonably respectable once more and got into clean garments, Fred too was beginning to see the funny side of the mishap.

Maggie swore she was sore for days afterwards with laughing, and being the sort of person she was, she made the most of the story when she met up with any of her cronies. Each time she told the story it improved on the previous time. At times she had difficulty controlling the laughter long enough to get the words out. Yes, those wir the days, the days o the 'ootside toilets'!

WUR BARN

Over a hundred years ago, a very enterprising and go ahead farmer in Rendall, William Brass, was putting in a lot of time and work in renovating his farm buildings.

In these times it was all stone work and in his case the roofs were being finished in welsh slate. These slates were not all the same colour, a few among them were a much more of a pale blue colour than the purplish shade of the majority.

Normally these would have been just slapped on randomly among the rest, but 'Da' was, if nothing else, a bit of an extrovert. He came up with the idea of using these odd coloured slates to put his own stamp on the building, by making his own initials W.B.

The roof was eventually finished, and duly admired by friends and neighbours alike when they visited the farm.

One individual however was none too bright, and looked in amazement at these blue initials on the roof. "Beuy, whut dis the W B mean?" he asked.

The farmer looked at him solemnly for a moment, before replying, "Dis thoo no see id for theesel beuy, that's 'wur barn'!"

ANITHER PIGGIE TALE

Thirs wan thing sure in ferming tales, the
    best anes for the price,
Concern the many episodes wi fermers an thir
    'grice'
This wan's no muckle different, concerns twa
    local lads,
Wha haed the kind o episode that git's passed
    on be dads.

Hid wis a blink o time ago, Tam hid cheus left
    the school,
An got a job wi Erchie, on his ferm at
    'Mucklepool'.
His duties they wir varied, some small an some
    quite big,
But in amang the many chores, Tam haed tae
    feed the pig.

Tam got on weel wi piggie, as he fed an
mucked him oot,
An bedded him in clean warm strae, for comfort
tae the brute.
The pig id saa in Tam a freen that cam in every
day,
Tae scratch id's aakward itchy bits, as he sheuk
oot the strae.

The hoose wis ould, an built o stone, a bittie fae
the ferm.
An hoosed a twa-tree strickies teu, tae keep
them oot o herm,
So Erchie popped in maist o days, tae see things
wir deun right,
An life sailed on sublimely as each day passed
intae night.

But aal good things come tae an end, wan day
Erchie decried,
"The time his come beuys tinks thoo no, this
pig needs tae be weighed!",
"If wae go tae id right awey, no whin wae hiv a
meenit,
Wae'll sort the job oot queekly, an be deun
afore wae ken it!"

So Erchie wi his wife Merro, an peedie Tam as
    weel,
Set forth intae the piggie's hoose, (you should
    hae haerd him squeal).
He didno like whin unkan folk disturbed his
    morning's rest,
An tried haerd tae man-hannel him an dreg him
    fae his nest.

He yelled an fought his very best, an tried haerd
    tae resist,
But wis maakan little heidwey, for them folk
    they wid persist.
He squirmed an he wriggled, hid meed him feel
    quite sore,
Tae be pushed aroond so carelessly, he spied the
    open door!

Wi wan last squeal o protest, an a wriggle o
    pure spite,
He broke awey fae aal o them, an heeded for
    the light,
An baet them aal oot tae the door, at last beuys
    he wis free!
He paused an haed a leuk aroond, so bright he
    couldno see.

78

Wi sunlight waarm apin his back, an wind soft
   on his skin
He thowt "This is the place for me, thirs no wey
   aam gaan in!"
He haed a peedie race aroond,"Hid's right
   graand tae be free!"
An set oot tae explore a bit, but "Drat id there's
   them three!"

"Hi Tam" shouts Erchie, "Heid him aaf, deu
   beuy cheus whut thoor bidden!"
The pig id swerved aroond them boath, an
   heided for the midden.
"Aal git him noo!" Tam yells oot queek, an teuk
   aaf in a dive.
Piggie saa Tam's fleean shadow, an deftly
   swung aside.

Poor lad he didno hiv a chance, tae think or
   reconnoitre.
Wan meenit fleean blissfally, nixt face doon in
   the iper!
The pig gaed dancan side-e-weys as Tam sank
   oot o sight
Tae rise a wiser chenged man, that really leuked
   a fright

Noo whin id comes tae ferming smells, there's
  nothing can compare
Wi rank an 'ripened' piggie muck, id really is
  "quite rare!"
Peur Tammie he wis coated, fae his beuts aap
  tae his heid
His lugs, eyes, even nostrils, wir aal weel filled
  indeed.

Hid hid clarted aap his pootches, an gaen aap
  boath his sleeves.
An seepid right trow tae his draars, so aam led
  tae believe.
They wiped him doon wi wisps o strae tae git
  him cleaned a bit.
But couldno taak awey the smell, o rank soor
  piggie s—t.

Hid teuk a while, but in a time they got thir
  piggie in.
Wance more intae hid's corner, whar he hid
  alwis been.
But Tam he wis a different case, he wis in saek
  a liper,
Wi pig muck stickan tae his face, an beuts still
  fill o iper.

He squelched his wey back tae the ferm, tae git
   his claes strip'd aaf.
An try tae git him scrubbid doon, hid's cheus no
   right tae laugh.
A bucket fae the byre door, warm watter fae the
   stove.
A scrubbing brush an bar o soap, tae git the dirt
   tae moave.

"Thir's no wey that he's coman in" wis Merro's
   warning words.
"Until he's more presentable, an free o aal them
   t—s"
So Tammie hid tae strip an waash afore the
   keetcheen door
Until he wis 'pollution free'an shinan bright
   wance more.

Weel, strippid doon tae socks an draars, he
   scrubbid manfully.
His face, his hair, ahint his lugs, wir seun aal
   'iper free'
He snushed an snorted, splashed aboot, than
   snushed an snorted more,
Until he wis wance more declared, 'fit tae come
   in the door'.

Noo Erchie teuk his byre fork, the claes tae tak
  right aaf,
Until they fund some kind o means tae shift the
  smelly stuff.
He dump'd id in the barrel ootside the byre
  door,
That seun smelt much, much, waer than hid hid
  ever smelt afore.

Noo Tam wis reckoned clean anof tae git intae a
  bath,
Tae aese the muck oot o his pores, an swulter
  hid right aaf.
Than got a change o Erchie's claes, although id
  didno fit,
Hid meed him daesant tae go home, tae git
  some ither kit.

Noo if you hae a bit o sense whin hearan o this
  tale,
An you hae 'grices' on your ferm, but dinna like
  the smell.
Mind whin you go tae weigh them up, be sure
  an close the door,
Or you could end aap laek Tammie, filled aap in
  every pore!

A GOLDEN OLDIE

A short story of doubtful origin is this one which I have heard many times, and with a number of settings.

Two rather eccentric brothers lived with their mother on an island croft. It has never been recorded whether they had at one time fallen out, but they seldom spoke to each other as they went about their duties. A grunt as they passed each other was about the height of their communication.

One day the younger one went out as normal, but he never returned. Time went on, a year passed then another, and yet another, and no word was heard of him. Then one day the door opened and in he walked, sat down in his favourite chair, hanging his cap on the corner as usual. His brother stared at him in some amazement for a long moment before he spoke, "Whar ir thoo been aal this time beuy?"

The wanderer barely glanced up as he replied, "Oot!

A RECORD MONTH

In Orkney the standard opening words in any conversation is a comment about the weather. If it happens to be good (not a normal occurrence), one must always look to the more gloomy side of things, "Faith beuy wae'll pay for this yit!" or some such remark. If it's bad, well you must always look for it to be worse. That way you never get caught out, by expecting too much in the way of good conditions.

Two neighbours met up one day, "Aye Robbo," commented the first,"hid's been a blashy twa weeks is id no!"

"Yass beuy," came the reply, "wunters no deun wi is yit I wad say!"

"Beuy, wae niver git a right wunter nooadays, weet an blash aal the time, no like the wunters wae hid whin wae wir boys!" said the first.

"Faith aye," came the response. "Fine dae I mind the ear, a whilie ago noo, wae hid a full six weeks o snow in the month o Merch!"

M E R C H

PHOTO R.M.BAIKIE   ORKNEY CAMERA CLUB

Sun	Mon	Tue	Wed	Thur	Fri	Sun
	1	2	3	4	5	6
7	8	9	10	11	12	13
14	15	16	17	18	19	20
21	22	23	24	25	26	27
28	29	30	31	32	33	34
35	36	37	38	39	40	41
42	43	44	45			

PITTAN OOT THE KYE

Wae ken hid is a trachle that comes roond
  every eer,
Whin the girs is green an lush an the fields aer
  bright wi breer,
Hid's been deun on the maist o ferms fae
  Adam wis a boy,
The eer's first sign o summer is the pittan oot
  the kye,
You'd think id wis 'idyllic' - traditional
  forbye,
This age old ferming based routine - this
  lowsing o the kye.
But noo things they aer chainchan, an
  progress mos be faced,
An things like pittan kye oot most be
  computer based.

'They' say no baes can be moved oot - unless
   id is permitted,
This his tae be applied for - an no wey should
   thoo forgit id,
For a weel paid man in Brussels kens more
   nor you an I,
That wance again the time his come, for pittan
   oot the kye.

Wan thing wae can be sure o noo whin kye go
   in a field,
Whin they git tae yir boundary, they ir duty
   bound tae yield.
No flighty stot or heifer noo can on your
   neebour stray,
Withoot they hae a permit that specifies the
   day.
Moavements mos be recorded an tae
   computers fed,
Should yir baes be runnan free, or fae the byre
   led.
Thirs no excuse accepted, hids cheus a lok o
   rot
Tae say thirs noathing thoo can deu tae stop a
   spooky stot.
Hid's in thir Brussels offece beuy, on
   computer, aye that's right,
Withoot yir 'movement record' beuy, no wey
   can they tak fright.

Hoo did they manage in the past? I'd really
like tae ken
Whin Grandad wis a peedie boy, an men wir
really men.
No records than, no c-c-d's, no 'passports'or
such tripe,
Each fermer pat his kye oot, whin he kent the
time wis right.
No stoopid 'moavement records', or ither
kinds o rot,
Laek clippan smelly pelters fae the belly o a
stot.
No things laek 'salmon-ella' than, 'E-colly' or
sic larks,
He hid twa days o 'coleeks' an cheus got on
wi his wark.
A speun or two o 'castor oil', or a grain o
'epsom sats',
An back he wis in working trim as sure is cats
is cats.

But noo tae move yir kye at aa, you mos git
word fae aaf,
Fae folk that ken no better, hid's anof tae mak
you laugh.
The day is near aboot thoo see's, whin thool
hae tae apply,
Aroond aboot September, tae pit kye oot in
Mey.
An whin thoo needs tae tak them in, thoo
really needs tae search
Tae git thee forms oot o the desk, tae fill them
in in Merch!

A CASE OF MISTAKEN IDENTITY

'Ould Ned' was one of the parish 'characters'. All his days he had been renowned for his sense of humour and his quick wit. Seldom had anyone ever been able to 'put one over' on Ned, though many had tried, to their cost and the amusement of others. Now a senior citizen, he remained as popular in the community as he had been during his younger days.

A farmer all his life, his retirement merely meant scaling down his farming to a couple of cows on his few remaining acres. These cows were cared for, petted and pampered as though they were members of his own family, and he put in many happy hours caring for their needs.

Cattle, as we know, need to be kept indoors during the long dark wet months of the Orkney winter. So in order to provide part of their daily diet, and to save on feed, Ned grew a patch of oats. He also made some hay in the summer months from surplus grass. Having no machinery of his own he relied on one or other of his neighbours to come along with a reaper or binder at the appropriate time of year, to cut his crop.

His payment was not with money, that was not the way things were done in those days. There were no contractors, no bills or the like, it was favour for favour in the time honoured way with him. Instead he went along to help these same neighbours with harvesting or the like, whenever he felt they could use a pair of extra hands. Besides he enjoyed the company of younger folk, and having these younger people around him joking and chatting added spice to his life, keeping his wits sharp.

One day Ned was at the neighbouring farm across the

valley from his own place, helping to stack oats. He was by a lifetime of experience an expert in this art, for such a job was truly a work of art, something we no longer see today on the farms.

This day he was fairly high up on the partly built stack when he stopped what he was doing and sat gazing away into the distance in the direction of his own holding. Making no comment he resumed his work, still casting the occasional glance into the distance.

Again he sat back, pushed back his cap and sat staring into the distance, before commenting to those who were there, "I think I wad need tae go home. Hid leuks like wan o me baes is gotten intae me aets! Aam been watchan id for a blink noo," he went on, "an ids no shiftan faer!"

The rest of the workers stopped as well to look across at his fields, but none could see anything out of the ordinary.

Still Ned went on adamantly, "That thing o a baes is definately in me aets, but ids bidan aafal weel aboot the saem piece. You folk can surely no see id fae doon there whar your staan!"

With another load of sheaves coming into the stackyard, work resumed as the discussion went on about what was to be done about this straying beast.

It was when the driver of the tractor arrived with his load builder, that the episode was resolved.

Ned appealed to the person on top of the load of sheaves, "Kin thoo see that baes o mine oot in me aets?" She looked, looked back at Ned, and looked into the distance again. "I see no baes oot there, thoo most be imaginan things beuy!"

"Ir thoo sure," was his puzzled response, "I dont ken whut wey thoo disno see id, id's as plain as can be tae me!"

"Weel," came the reply, "I see no baes near thee aets, aal I see is a burd, a craa or something sittan on the 'Hydro' line!"

There was a long silence as every one looked at the scene. Sure enough there were a couple of birds on the distant line, some distance apart. One of these was in the right place to possibly be confused for 'a baes' by an older eye.

Poor Ned, finally he had to admit with the greatest of reluctance that he was mistaken for once. He too being always ready for a 'fun', could appreciate the humour in the situation, and shared in the laughter. But from that day on, there was no more boasting about his 'baes' being "faer better or anything thool see at the shows!"

"Efter aal beuy, thoo canno tell the difference atween thee baes an a ould craa!" was the usual comment thrown at him by those who had shared the joke.

I'm sure he enjoyed the laugh as much as the rest, and no doubt had many a quiet chuckle to himself afterwards whenever it came into his mind.

He was that sort of a man.

WILD WARK

Another North Isles story I heard many years ago relates
to a farm where quite a number of cattle were outwintered
regularly. Though they were used to being fed and cared for
on a routine basis, there was a streak of wildness in these
beasts that is not found so much in housed stock. Some of
these were of Galloway stock, and a few were pure Highland,
complete with the wide spreading horns these cattle are
famous for.

Winter passed into spring and some of the cows produced
calves on the links where they were lying. There were few
problems with this natural process, and things were going
smoothly. But as the land dried out, and spring grass started
to cover the fields, the farmer decided the time had come to
move them into a park nearer the house. As any farmer
knows there can be a problem from time to time at birth, and
it's better to get assistance quickly, rather than too late. This
farm, in common with many others of the period, had large

square walled fields, which could provide reasonable shelter from the worst of the elements in typically unsettled spring weather.

The farm was a big one with a couple of servant men employed full time on the place. The older one had spent his working life on the farm and worked it almost as if it were his own property. The second man was experienced in all aspects of work as well but was a good twenty five years younger.

It was this more youthful man who became the one unwittingly involved in this episode.

While his senior partner worked with the stock in the farm buildings, 'Tam' with his tractor and box went the rounds of the outside stock, checking and feeding them as required.

He was used to working with these outside cattle and they knew him well enough to trust him as he worked among them.

One morning, having set out at first light to check whether there had been any new arrivals during the night, he found one 'Highlander'was having a problem pushing out a big calf.

Having thought only for the welfare of the cow and calf, he went to her assistance, and after a lot of pulling and sweating on both their parts a strong bull calf was delivered.

"They should be fine now," he thought, standing back to put on his jacket and noticing at the same time that they were lying close to a sheltering stone dyke surrounding the field.

Before he knew what was happening, the cow sprang to her feet, and with eyes blazing and head down charged him. Quickly, for his own protection, he grabbed the stones on top of the wall and jumped over it to safety - or so he thought!

Next he knew those sweeping horns caught the calf and slung it over the wall almost on top of him. Before he had time to think or react, the cow herself cleared the wall also to land beside the calf.

Seeing him standing there, she again turned her attention to him, so over the wall he went again - followed seconds later by the calf.

Again the cow clambered over the wall, and the process repeated itself two or three times. Each time he jumped the wall the cow tossed the calf after him, or so it appeared.

It seemed the enraged cow was venting her feelings on anything that moved.

After what appeared to him to be half a day, Tam eventually managed to get back to the safety of his tractor. Afterwards he assured every one he had cleared the wall six times at the very least, each time from a standing start.

Surprisingly enough the calf had not come to any obvious harm from this onslaught, and when the mother cooled down she was as caring and attentive as any mother could be with her young.

No doubt it was the presence of a man on the scene which caused her to go berserk in the first place. If things had been normal, she would no doubt have quietly gone about attending to her calf in a routine fashion.

WAN FOR THE POT

A lad lived on a North Isles ferm, hid deun fae
  he wis born
He learned so many usefal things, like hoo the
  sheep wir shorn.
At calfan coos, an lamban yowes, he seun
  could turn his hand
Or in the boat at evening, catchan sillicks wi a
  wand.

He learned things in the age old wey, be
  watchan whut wis deen
An tryan haerd tae copy, the things that he hid
  seen,
He seun became an expert at maist o common
  chores,
Be it bucket feedan calves, or dreggan ware
  aap fae the shore.

Wan day as he wis settan oot, a walk doon tae
    the shore,
Tae feed the batch o layan hens, that hid been
    there fae vore.
His mither cried oot fae the door, sheu saa him
    settan oot,
"Thinks thoo beuy can thoo grip a hen, wae
    need ane for the pot!"

Noo as wae ken this really means, you need tae
    wring id's neck,
But this wur lad hid never deun, still he knew
    whut tae expect.
The hens wir runnan haerd tae meet him, wey
    up across the field,
He thought "If I cheus grab ane noo, aal be a
    clever chiel".

"Sheu'll lie here till I come back home, hid'll
    save a bit o cairry,"
"A long waak back up tae the hoose'll mak her
    kindo heavy!"
So waitan there aside the dyke, the hens aal
    gaethered roond,
He flietered in among them, an grabbed wan
    fat an broon.

Noo this is whar he cam unstuck, his
knowledge let him doon,
"Hoo dae you wring a burdie's neck, whut's
flappan aap an doon?"
He teuk his time an hid a think, hoo hid he
seen hid deun ?
"The heid atween thee fingers beuy, than twurl
the body roon!"

But his grip hid wisno tight anof, aroon the
creatur's neck,
The hen teuk wan almighty heave, an flew aaf
wi a skrek.
Wi flappan weengs, an stridan legs, sheu teuk
aaf for the shore,
Like 'nick' himsel wis efter her, an strainan
every pore.

Poor chap he hidno any choice but stramp
across the field,
An feed the lot as wis his wont, they wirno
gaan tae yield.
Mistrust hid glowed in every eye, they
watched his every motion,
No hen cam tae within his reach, they viewed
him wi suspeecion.

He hid no choice, wi empty hand, but tae
  return home,
Wi nothing for the dinner pot, tae fill an empty
  tum.
Till faither gaed oot tae the shed an fund
  anither burd,
An shaad him hoo tae deu the job, (this really
  is absurd)

But fae that day tae this ane, the lad his no
  forgot,
His first attempt tae grip a hen, tae pit in
  mither's pot.
He's noo a man o many years, but still minds
  o the shame
O coman home tae tell his mam he couldno
  'grip a hen'.

THE MOOTHLESS MAN

It's not only men who get caught out in some embarrassing situations. The fair sex are also prone to get caught out, it would be safe to assume, at least after hearing the tale here.

Meg was a widow, and had lived on her own for many years. Her small cottage had a few acres of land around it which she liked to look after as best she could, even though she was not farming it.

A neighbour, Tam, had use of this plot of land for grazing a couple of cows, which had to be tethered as there was no fence.

He went along daily to check them, move them when necessary to a fresh patch, and give them a drink.

One day though, Meg noticed that one of Tam's cows had got loose. On investigating she discovered the stake had been pulled from the ground. Even though the cow was not near where she had been, Meg got the stake driven into the ground again to secure the beast.

It was a fine day and as Tam's croft was only about a quarter of a mile along the road, she decided to walk over and tell him what had happened. She could after all see him out working in his 'neep' field!

What she was unaware of was that Tam had been having trouble with hares and rabbits attacking his 'neeps'. In an attempt to discourage their activities he had spent some time rigging up a lifelike scarecrow, complete with 'kep' and an old raincoat.

Meg, always a ready talker came along the road, and as she came to within calling distance shouted out to this 'man' in the 'neep' field, "Aye Tam, I see thoor busy the day!" She got no response.

Moving a bit nearer, she called out again, "Beuy Tam, thoor surely no hearan me the day!" Again no response.

Puzzled now and not a little annoyed, she came on, telling her story as she came, knowing full well that Tam was now well within hearing distance.

It was only as she came closer that she realised that she was trying to hold a conversation with a very well made dummy. Little wonder she got no response.

Having been blessed with a good sense of humour she could see the funny side of the situation, and was still chuckling to herself as she reached the farm steading.

Over the usual cup of tea and a biscuit this story came to light, much to the amusement of Tam and his family.

They thought it was a hilarious story and many a time it has been told and retold as the years have passed.

EVIL SPIRITS

Many years ago there was an elderly crofter living out in the East Mainland. He lived alone, and was regarded as something of an eccentric in the parish. Like many elderly bachelors he loved the occasional dram. "Hid helps thee sleep at night, thoo sees!" was a favourite expression.

Like others of his generation, his trips to town were few, and usually driven by necessity. His transport on such occasions was his elderly pony and trap. This pony like its master had lived for years on the same place, and could find its way home on its own in any sort of conditions when necessary.

A very useful thing too, for when Dave went to town, he was usually incapable of driving all the way home after a few rounds with 'Johnnie Walker'.

The youth of the parish, as in any other, were always ready for any bit of new entertainment to liven up their evenings. They were well aware of Dave and his habits, often watching every step with amusement, as he and his pony returned from their trips to town.

One evening, it was a beautifully still moonlight night, when the parish grapevine buzzed with the news that Dave was on his way back from town "Wi a good shot in!"

A number of these young bloods very quickly decided among themselves to "Hiv a peedie fun wi Dave."

His route meant that he had to drive past the local kirkyard on his way home, so they thought up an idea to give him the fright of his life.

Gathering together a number of white or light coloured bed sheets, they congregated among the grave stones to wait.

Eventually the pony and trap appeared trundling unhurriedly along the moonlit road. As they came near the graveyard, first one and then another white sheeted figure rose from among the grave stones to line along the wall and wave at the travellers.

Totally unconcerned, Dave and his pony plodded onwards!

As he reached the last in line of these ghostly figures along the churchyard wall, he was heard to ask in a somewhat slurred voice, "Yaas beuys, is this a general uprising? Or is id cheus twatree o you needan tae git aap for a pee?"